Cowboy Boots

SKILL LEVEL

◼◼◼◻
INTERMEDIATE

FINISHED SIZES

Instructions given fit child's shoe size small (7–10); changes for child's medium (11–13) and large (1–3) and adult's small (women's 5–6), medium (women's 7–8), large (women's 9–10/ men's 7–9) and X-large (men's 10–13) are in [ ].

FINISHED MEASUREMENTS

Sole: 6¾ [7½, 8½, 9, 9¾, 10½, 11¾] inches

MATERIALS

- Medium (worsted) weight yarn: 6⅝ oz/330 yds/187g gold (A) 4½ oz/225 yds/128g light brown (B)
- Sizes H/8/5mm, I/9/5.5mm and J/10/6mm crochet hooks or size needed to obtain gauge
- 2 stitch markers
- Tapestry needle

GAUGE

Size H hook: 5 sc = 1¾ inches; 6 sc rows = 1¾ inches
Size I hook: 6 sc = 2 inches; 6 sc rows = 2 inches
Size J hook: 8 sc and 8 rows = 3 inches
Take time to check gauge.

PATTERN NOTES

Some sizes are achieved by changing the hook size, but the stitch count is the same as other sizes.

Boots are worked with 2 strands held together unless otherwise stated.

It will always look as if you are skipping a stitch or two at the end of each round. They are the joining slip stitch and chain-1. Do not work in these.

The stitch counts in [ ] may not always be in numerical sequence. These numbers are correct.

Join with slip stitch as indicated unless otherwise stated.

COWBOY BOOT
MAKE 2.
SOLE
Rnd 1: With H [J, J, I, J, J, J] hook and with B, ch 13 [13, 15, 18, 18, 21, 24], 2 sc in 2nd ch from hook, sc in each of next 6 [6, 7, 9, 9, 11, 13] chs, dc in each of next 3 [3, 4, 5, 5, 6, 7] chs, 2 dc in next ch, 5 dc in end ch, mark center dc for toe, working in rem lps across opposite side of starting ch, 2 dc in next st, dc in each of next 3 [3, 4, 5, 5, 6, 7] sts, sc in each of next 7 [7, 8, 10, 10, 12, 14] sts, **join** *(see Pattern Notes)* in first sc. *(15 [15, 16, 21, 21, 25, 29] sc, 15 [15, 17, 19, 19, 21, 23] dc)*

CHILD SMALL, MEDIUM & LARGE AND ADULT SMALL & MEDIUM SIZES ONLY
Rnd 2 [2, 2, 2, 2]: Ch 1, sc in same st, 2 sc in next st, sc in each of next 12 [12, 14, 17, 17] sts, 2 sc in next st, 3 sc in next st, 2 sc in next st, sc in each of next 12 [12, 14, 17, 17] sts, 2 sc in next st, join in first sc. *(36 [36, 40, 46, 46] sc)*

ADULT LARGE & X-LARGE SIZES ONLY
Rnd [2, 2]: Ch 1, sc in same st, 2 sc in next st, sc in each of next [8, 9] sts, hdc in each of next [6, 7] sts, dc in each of next [6, 7] sts, 2 dc in next st, 3 dc in next st, 2 dc in next st, dc in each of next [6, 7] sts, hdc in each of next [6, 7] sts, sc in each of next [8, 9] sts, 2 sc in next st, join in first sc. *([21, 23] sc, [12, 14] hdc, [19, 21] dc)*

ALL SIZES
Rnd 3 [3, 3, 3, 3, 3, 3]: Ch 1, sc in same st, 2 sc in next st, sc in each of next 12 [12, 14, 17, 17, 20, 23] sts, [2 sc in next st, sc in each of next 3 sts] twice, 2 sc in next st, sc in each of next 12 [12, 14, 17, 17, 20, 23] sts, 2 sc in next st, join in first sc. Fasten off. *(41 [41, 45, 51, 51, 57, 63] sts)*

HEEL
With toe pointing away, sk 6 [6, 7, 8, 8, 9, 10] sts to right of fastened off st and place marker, with B and working in **back lps** *(see Stitch Guide)*, join in marked st, sc in each of next 3 [3, 4, 4, 5, 5] sts, hdc in each of next 5 [5, 5, 7, 7, 7, 9] sts, move marker to center hdc, sc in each of next 3 [3, 4, 4, 4, 5, 5] sts, join in next st. Fasten off.

TOP
Rnd 1: With A, join with a sc in back lp of marked Heel st, working in back lps only, sc in each of next 17 [17, 18, 20, 20, 22, 24], hdc in each of next 6 [6, 8, 10, 10, 12, 14] sts, sc in each of next 17 [17, 18, 20, 20, 22, 24] sts, join in first sc.

Rnd 2: Ch 1, sc in same st, sc in each of next 11 [11, 13, 16, 16, 16, 19] sts, sk next st, hdc in next st, dc in next st, [**dc dec** *(see Stitch Guide)* in next 2 sts, dc in next st] 2 [2, 2, 2, 2, 3, 3] times, [dc in next st, dc dec in next st] 2 [2, 2, 2, 2, 3, 3] times, dc in next st, hdc in next st, sk next st, sc in each of next 11 [11, 13, 16, 16, 16, 19] sts, join in first sc. *(35 [35, 39, 45, 45, 49, 55] sts)*

Rnd 3: Ch 1, sc in same st, sc in each of next 11 [11, 13, 16, 16, 15, 18] sts, [dc dec in next 2 sts, dc in next st] 2 [2, 2, 2, 2, 3, 3] times, [dc in next st, dc dec in next 2 sts] 2 [2, 2, 2, 2, 3, 3] times, sc in each of next 11 [11, 13, 16, 16, 15, 18], join in first sc. *(31 [31, 35, 41, 41, 43, 49] sts)*

Rnd 4: Ch 1, sc in same st, sc in each of next 9 [9, 11, 14, 14, 15, 18] sts, [dc dec in next 2 sts, dc in next st] twice, [dc in next st, dc dec in next 2 sts] twice, sc in each of next 9 [9, 11, 14, 14, 15, 18] sts, join in first sc. *(27 [27, 31, 37, 37, 39, 45] sts)*

Rnd 5: Ch 1, sc in same st, sc in each of next 7 [7, 9, 12, 12, 13, 16] sts, [dc dec in next 2 sts, dc in next st] twice, [dc in next st, dc dec in next 2 sts] twice, sc in each of next 7 [7, 9, 12, 12, 13, 16] sts, join in first sc. *(23 [23, 27, 33, 33, 35, 41] sts)*

CHILD SMALL, MEDIUM & LARGE SIZES ONLY
Rnd 6 [6, 6]: Ch 1, sc in same st, sc in each of next 5 [5, 7] sts, [**sc dec** *(see Stitch Guide)* in next 2 sts, sc in next st] twice, [sc in next st, sc dec in next 2 sts] twice, sc in each of next 5 [5, 7] sts, join in first sc. Fasten off. *(19 [19, 23] sts)*

ADULT SMALL, MEDIUM, LARGE & X-LARGE SIZES ONLY

Rnd [6, 6, 6, 6]: Ch 1, sc in same st, sc in each of next [10, 10, 11, 14] sts, **sc dec** (see Stitch Guide) in next 2 sts, dc in next st, dc dec in next 2 sts, dc in each of next 2 dc, dc dec in next 2 sts, dc in next st, dc dec in next 2 sts, sc in each of next [10, 10, 11, 14] sts, join in first sc. ([29, 29, 31, 37] sts)

Rnd [7, 7, 7, 7]: Ch 1, sc in same st, sc in each of next [8, 8, 9, 12] sts, [sc dec in next 2 sts, sc in next st] twice, [sc in next st, sc dec in next 2 sts] twice, sc in each of next [8, 8, 9, 12] sts, join in first sc.

ADULT SMALL, MEDIUM & LARGE SIZES ONLY

Fasten off. ([25, 25, 27] sts)

ADULT X-LARGE SIZE ONLY

Rnd [8]: Ch 1, sc in same st, sc in each of next 10 sts, [dc dec in next 2 sts, sc in next st] twice, [sc in next st, dc dec in next 2 sts] twice, sc in each of next 10 sts, join in first sc. Fasten off. ([29] sts)

LEG OF BOOT

Rnd 1: With B and working in back lp only for this rnd, join with sc in same st where you just fastened off, sc in each st around, join in first sc. (19 [19, 23, 25, 25, 27, 29] sts)

Rnd 2: Ch 1, sc in same st, sc in each st around, join in top of first sc.

Next rnds: Rep rnd 2 11 [11, 12, 13, 13, 14, 15] times.

Last rnd: Ch 1, sc in same st, sc in each of next 2 [2, 3, 4, 4, 5, 7] sts, sk next st, dc in next st, 3 dc in each of next 2 sts, dc in next st, sk 1 st, sc in each of next 4 [4, 7, 8, 8, 9, 9] sts, sk next st, dc in next st, 3 dc in each of next 2 sts, dc in next st, sk next st, join in first sc. Fasten off. (23 [23, 27, 29, 29, 31, 33] sts)

TRIM

With A, join with sc at center back, sc in each st, with 2 sc in middle dc of each 3-dc group on last rnd, join in first sc. Fasten off.

Rep on rem Boot.

FRONT EMBLEM
MAKE 2.

Row 1: With A, working in **front lps** (see Stitch Guide), sc in each of 3 center front sts of toe of Boot.

Rows 2–4: Ch1, sc in each of next 3 sc, turn.

Row 5: Ch 1, (sc, hdc) in first sc, 3 dc in next sc, (hdc, sc) in next sc. Fasten off.

Tack top of 1 Emblem to each Boot Leg.

SIDE DECORATION

With single strand of A, ch 40. Arrange in design as shown in illustration and tack in place. Rep on rem Boot.

Cowboy Boots
Decoration on Sides Placement Diagram

SOLE RIDGE

Remove stitch markers.

With B, join at center back of heel in front lp only, sl st loosely in front lp only of each st around. Join and fasten off.

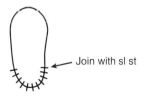

← Join with sl st

Cowboy Boots
Heel Joining Diagram

Rep on rem Boot.

FINISHING

Weave in all ends and remove stitch markers. ■

High-Top Tennies

SKILL LEVEL

INTERMEDIATE

FINISHED SIZES
Instructions given fit child's shoe size small (7–10); changes for child's medium (11–13) and large (1–3) and adult's small (women's 5–6), medium (women's 7–8), large (women's 9–10/ men's 7–9) and X-large (men's 10–13) are in [ ].

FINISHED MEASUREMENTS
Sole: 6¾ [7½, 8½, 9, 9¾, 10½, 11¾] inches

MATERIALS
- Medium (worsted) weight yarn:
  4⅛ oz/210 yds/119g black *(A)*
  3½ oz/180 yds/102g white *(B)*
  ⅝ oz/32 yds/18g red *(C)*
- Sizes H/8/5mm, I/9/5.5mm and J/10/6mm crochet hooks or size needed to obtain gauge
- Stitch markers
- Tapestry needle

GAUGE
Size H hook: 5 sc = 1¾ inches; 6 sc rows = 1¾ inches
Size I hook: 6 sc = 2 inches; 6 sc rows = 2 inches
Size J hook: 8 sc and 8 rows = 3 inches
Take time to check gauge.

PATTERN NOTES
Some sizes are achieved by changing the hook size, but the stitch count is the same as other sizes.

Tennies are worked with 2 strands held together unless otherwise stated.

Divide each skein into two evenly sized hand-wound balls.

It will always look as if you are skipping a stitch or two at the end of each round. They are the joining slip stitch and chain-1. Do not work in these.

The stitch counts in [ ] may not always be in numerical sequence. These numbers are correct.

Join with slip stitch as indicated unless otherwise stated.

HIGH-TOP TENNIES
MAKE 2.
SOLE
Rnd 1: With H [J, J, I, J, J, J] hook and with B, ch 13 [13, 15, 18, 18, 21, 24], 2 sc in 2nd ch from hook, sc in each of next 6 [6, 7, 9, 9, 11, 13] chs, dc in each of next 3 [3, 4, 5, 5, 6, 7] chs, 2 dc in next ch, 5 dc in end ch, mark center dc for toe, working in rem lps across opposite side of

starting ch, 2 dc in next st, dc in each of next 3 [3, 4, 5, 5, 6, 7] sts, sc in each of next 7 [7, 8, 10, 10, 12, 14] sts, **join** *(see Pattern Notes)* in first sc. *(15 [15, 16, 21, 21, 25, 29] sc, 15 [15, 17, 19, 19, 21, 23] dc)*

CHILD SMALL, MEDIUM, LARGE & ADULT SMALL & MEDIUM SIZES ONLY

Rnd 2 [2, 2, 2, 2]: Ch 1, sc in same st, 2 sc in next st, sc in each of next 12 [12, 14, 17, 17] sts, 2 sc in next st, 3 sc in next st, 2 sc in next st, sc in each of next 12 [12, 14, 17, 17] sts, 2 sc in next st, join in first sc. *(36 [36, 40, 46, 46] sc)*

ADULT LARGE & X-LARGE SIZES ONLY

Rnd [2, 2]: Ch 1, sc in same st, 2 sc in next st, sc in each of next [8, 9] sts, hdc in each of next [6, 7] sts, dc in each of next [6, 7] sts, 2 dc in next st, 3 dc in next st, 2 dc in next st, dc in each of next [6, 7] sts, hdc in each of next [6, 7] sts, sc in each of next [8, 9] sts, 2 sc in next st, join in first sc. *([21, 23] sc, [12, 14] hdc, [19, 21] dc)*

ALL SIZES

Rnd 3 [3, 3, 3, 3, 3, 3]: Ch 1, sc in same st, 2 sc in next st, sc in each of next 12 [12, 14, 17, 17, 20, 23] sts, [2 sc in next st, sc in each of next 3 sts] twice, 2 sc in next st, sc in each of next 12 [12, 14, 17, 17, 20, 23] sts, 2 sc in next st, join in first sc. Fasten off. *(41 [41, 45, 51, 51, 57, 63] sts)*

UPPER SOLE

Rnd 1: Working in **back lps** *(see Stitch Guide)*, for this rnd, with C, join in fastened off st from previous rnd, ch 1, sc in same st, sc in each st around, join in first sc. Fasten off.

Rnd 2: Working in back lps, with B, join in fastened off st from previous rnd, ch 1, sc in same st, sc in each st around, join in first sc. Fasten off.

TOE PIECE

Row 1: Now working in rows, sk next 14 [14, 15, 16, 16, 19, 22] sts, with B, join in next st, working all sts in back lps for this row, sc in next st, sk next st, dc in each of next 2 [2, 1, 1, 1, 1, 1] st(s), **dc dec** *(see Stitch Guide)* in next 2 sts 1 [1, 3, 5, 5, 5, 5] time(s), dc in each of next 2 [2, 1, 1, 1, 1, 1] st(s), sk next st, sc in next st, join in next st. Fasten off.

TONGUE
CHILD SMALL, MEDIUM & LARGE SIZES ONLY

Row 1 [1, 1]: With A and working in back lps only for this row, join with sc in first sc of Toe Piece, sc in each of next 6 sts, turn.

Row 2 [2, 2]: Ch 1, sc in each of next 7 sts, turn.

Row 3 [3, 3]: Ch 1, sk first sc, sc in each of next 6 sts, turn.

Row 4 [4, 4]: Ch 1, sk first sc, sc in each of next 5 sts, turn.

Rows 5 & 6 [5 & 6, 5 & 6]: Ch 1, sc in each of next 5 sts, turn.

Row 7 [7, 7]: Ch 1, sk first sc, sc in each of next 4 sts, turn.

Rows 8–13 [8–13, 8–13]: Ch 1, sc in each of next 4 sts, turn. Fasten off after last row.

ADULT SMALL, MEDIUM, LARGE & X-LARGE SIZES ONLY

Row [1, 1, 1, 1]: With A and working in back lps only for this row, join with sc in first sc of Toe Piece, sc in each of next 8 sts, turn.

Rows [2–5, 2–5, 2–5, 2–5]: Ch 1, sc in each of next 9 sts, turn.

Row [6, 6, 6, 6]: Ch 1, sk first st, sc in each of next 8 sts, turn.

Rows [7 & 8, 7 & 8, 7 & 8, 7 & 8]: Ch 1, sc in each of next 8 sts, turn.

Row [9, 9, 9, 9]: Ch 1, sk first sc, sc in each of next 7 sts, turn.

Rows [10 & 11, 10 & 11, 10 & 11, 10 & 11]: Ch 1, sc in each of next 7 sts, turn.

Row [12, 12, 12, 12]: Ch 1, sk first sc, sc in each of next 6 sts, turn.

Rows [13–16, 13–16, 13–18, 13–20]: Ch 1, sc in each of next 6 sts, turn. Fasten off after last row.

SHOE

Row 1: With A and working in back lp of rnd 2 sts of Upper Sole, join with sc in same st as last sl st of Toe Piece, sc in each sc around, sc in same st as first sl st of Toe Piece, turn. *(31 [31, 33, 35, 35, 41, 47] sts at end of last row)*

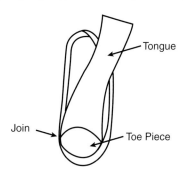

High-Top Tennies
Tongue Placement Diagram

Rows 2–7 [2–7, 2–7, 2–7, 2–7, 2–9, 2–11]: Sk first sc, sc in each st across to last 2 sts, **sc dec** *(see Stitch Guide)* in next 2 sts, turn. *(19 [19, 21, 23, 23, 25, 27] sts at end of last row)*

Rows 8–10 [8–10, 8–10, 8–12, 8–12, 10–12, 12–14]: Ch 1, sc in each sc, turn.

Fasten off.

TRIM ROW

With B, sc in each sc of last row. Fasten off.

RIDGE AROUND SOLE

Working this rnd into rem lps of rnd 3 of Sole, with Sole facing away from you, and with B, join with sl st at center back of heel, sl st loosely in each st around. Join and fasten off.

CIRCLES
MAKE 4.

With single strand of B, ch 4, 10 dc in 4th ch from hook, join in top of ch 4. Fasten off. Tack 1 Circle to each side of each Shoe.

SHOE STRINGS
MAKE 2.

With single strand of B, ch 110 [110, 115, 120, 120, 125, 130]. Fasten off. Lace into front edges and tie.

FINISHING

Weave in all ends and remove stitch markers. ∎

Track Shoes

SKILL LEVEL

■■■□
INTERMEDIATE

FINISHED SIZES

Instructions given fit child's shoe size small
  (7–10); changes for child's medium (11–13),
  large (1–3), and adult's small (women's 5–6),
  medium (women's 7–8), large (women's 9–10/
  men's 7–9) and X-large (men's 10–13) are in [ ].

FINISHED MEASUREMENTS

Sole: 6¾ [7½, 8½, 9, 9¾, 10½, 11¾] inches

MATERIALS

- Medium (worsted) weight yarn:
  3⅝ oz/181 yds/103g gold (A)
  3½ oz/175 yds/99g white (C)
  3⅜ oz/120 yds/96g royal blue (B)
- Sizes H/8/5mm, I/9/5.5mm and J/10/6mm
  crochet hooks or size needed to obtain gauge
- Stitch marker
- Tapestry needle

GAUGE

Size H hook: 5 sc = 1¾ inches; 6 sc rows =
  1¾ inches
Size I hook: 6 sc = 2 inches; 6 sc rows = 2 inches
Size J hook: 8 sc and 8 rows = 3 inches
Take time to check gauge.

PATTERN NOTES

Some sizes are achieved by changing the hook size,
  but the stitch count is the same as other sizes.

Shoes are worked with 2 strands of yarn held
  together throughout unless otherwise stated.

Divide each skein into two evenly sized hand-
  wound balls.

It will always look as if you are skipping a stitch
  or two at the end of each round; they are the
  joining slip stitch and chain 1; do not work
  in these.

The stitch counts in [ ] may not always be in
  numerical sequence. These numbers are correct.

SPECIAL STITCH

2-double crochet cluster (2-dc cl): Holding back
  last lp of each st on hook, 2 dc in indicated st or
  sp, yo, draw through all 3 lps on hook.

TRACK SHOE
MAKE 2.
SOLE

Rnd 1: With H [J, J, I, J, J, J] hook and with A, ch 13 [13, 15, 18, 18, 21, 24], 2 sc in 2nd ch from hook, sc in each of next 6 [6, 7, 9, 9, 11, 13] chs, dc in each of next 3 [3, 4, 5, 5, 6, 7] chs, 2 dc in next ch, 5 dc in end ch, mark center dc for toe, working in rem lps across opposite side of starting ch, 2 dc in next st, dc in each of next 3 [3, 4, 5, 5, 6, 7] sts, sc in each of next 7 [7, 8, 10, 10, 12, 14] sts, **join** (see Pattern Notes) in first sc. (15 [15, 16, 21, 21, 25, 29] sc, 15 [15, 17, 19, 19, 21, 23] dc)

CHILD SMALL, MEDIUM & LARGE AND ADULT SMALL & MEDIUM SIZES ONLY

Rnd 2 [2, 2, 2, 2]: Ch 1, sc in same st, 2 sc in next st, sc in each of next 12 [12, 14, 17, 17] sts, 2 sc in next st, 3 sc in next st, 2 sc in next st, sc in each of next 12 [12, 14, 17, 17] sts, 2 sc in next st, join in first sc. (36 [36, 40, 46, 46] sc)

ADULT LARGE & X-LARGE SIZES ONLY

Rnd [2, 2]: Ch 1, sc in same st, 2 sc in next st, sc in each of next [8, 9] sts, hdc in each of next [6, 7] sts, dc in each of next [6, 7] sts, 2 dc in next st, 3 dc in next st, 2 dc in next st, dc in each of next [6, 7] sts, hdc in each of next [6, 7] sts, sc in each of next [8, 9] sts, 2 sc in next st, join in first sc. ([21, 23] sc, [12, 14] hdc, [19, 21] dc)

ALL SIZES

Rnd 3 [3, 3, 3, 3, 3, 3]: Ch 1, sc in same st, 2 sc in next st, sc in each of next 12 [12, 14, 17, 17, 20, 23] sts, [2 sc in next st, sc in each of next 3 sts] twice, 2 sc in next st, sc in each of next 12 [12, 14, 17, 17, 20, 23] sts, 2 sc in next st, join in first sc. (41 [41, 45, 51, 51, 57, 63] sts)

Rnd 4 [4, 4, 4, 4, 4, 4]: Working in **back lps** (see Stitch Guide), ch 1, sc in same st, sc in each of next 16 [16, 17, 20, 20, 22, 24] sts, hdc in each of next 2 sts, dc in each of next 4 [4, 6, 6, 6, 8, 10] sts, hdc in each of next 2 sts, sc in each of next 16 [16, 17, 20, 20, 22, 24] sts, join in first sc. Fasten off.

SHOE
ADULT SMALL, MEDIUM, LARGE & X-LARGE SIZES ONLY

Rnd [1, 1, 1, 1]: With B and working in back lps only for this rnd, join with sc in last st of previous row, sc in each st around, join in first sc.

ALL SIZES

Rnd 1 [1, 1, 2, 2, 2, 2]: Ch 1, sc in same st, sc in each of next 17 [17, 16, 16, 16, 19, 19] sts, [**sc dec** (see Stitch Guide) in next 2 sts, sc in next st] 1 [1, 2, 3, 3, 3, 4] time(s), [sc in next st, sc dec in next 2 sts] 1 [1, 2, 3, 3, 3, 4] time(s), sc in each of next 17 [17, 16, 16, 16, 19, 19] sts, join in first sc. (39 [39, 41, 45, 45, 51, 55] sts)

Rnd 2 [2, 2, 3, 3, 3, 3]: Ch 1, sc in same st, sc in each of next 13 [13, 14, 13, 13, 16, 18] sts, [**sc dec** (see Stitch Guide) in next 2 sts, sc in next st] 2 [2, 2, 3, 3, 3, 3] times, [sc in next st, sc dec in next 2 sts] 2 [2, 2, 3, 3, 3, 3] times, sc in each of next 13 [13, 14, 13, 13, 16, 18] sts, join in first sc. (35 [35, 37, 39, 39, 45, 49] sts)

Rnd 3 [3, 3, 4, 4, 4, 4]: Ch 1, sc in same st, sc in each of next 11 [11, 12, 13, 13, 15, 18] sts, [sc dec in next 2 sts, sc in next st] twice, [sc in next st twice, sc dec in next 2 sts] twice, sc in each of next 11 [11, 12, 13, 13, 15, 18] sts, join in first sc. Fasten off. (31 [31, 33, 35, 35, 41, 45] sts)

INSTEP
CHILD SMALL, MEDIUM & LARGE SIZES ONLY

Row 1 [1, 1]: Now working in rows with C, work in back lps only of front middle 6 sts from last rnd, opposite toe marker, join in first st, [sc dec in next 2 sts] twice, sl st in next st, turn.

Rows 2 & 3 [2 & 3, 2 & 3]: Ch 1, sc in each sc, turn.

Row 4 [4, 4]: Ch 1, 2 sc in first sc, sc in next st, turn.

Row 5 [5, 5]: Ch 1, 2 sc in first sc, sc in each of next 2 sts. Fasten off.

ADULT SMALL, MEDIUM, LARGE & X-LARGE SIZES ONLY

Row [1, 1, 1, 1]: Now working in rows, join C in back lp of first of front middle 6 sts from last rnd, opposite toe marker, working in back lps, sl st in first st, sc in each of next 4 sts, sl st in 6th st, turn.

Rows [2 & 3, 2 & 3, 2–4, 2–4]: Ch 1, sc in each of next 4 sts across, turn.

Row [4, 4, 5, 5]: Ch 1, sc in each of first 2 sc, 2 sc in next st, sc in next st, turn.

Row [5, 5, 6, 6]: Ch 1, sc in each of first 3 sc, 2 sc in next sc, sc in next sc, turn.

ADULT SMALL, MEDIUM & LARGE SIZES ONLY

Row [6, 6, 7]: Ch 1, sc in each st across. Fasten off.

ADULT X-LARGE SIZE ONLY

Rows [7]: Ch 1, sc in each st across. Fasten off.

STOCKING
ALL SIZES

Rnd 1: Now working in rnds, with C and working in back lps only for this rnd, join with sc in same st where you fastened off on last rnd of shoe, sc in each of next 8 [8, 9, 10, 10, 11, 12] sts, sc in each of next 4 [4, 4, 6, 6, 6, 6] sts across Instep, sc in each of last 8 [8, 9, 10, 10, 11, 12] sts before first sc of rnd, join in first sc.

Rnd 2: Ch 1, sc in same st, sc in each st around, working sc dec in 2 sts on each side of Instep, join in first sc. (19, [19, 21, 25, 25, 27, 29] sts)

ADULT SMALL, MEDIUM, LARGE & X-LARGE SIZES ONLY

Rnd [3, 3, 3, 3]: Rep rnd 2. ([23, 23, 25, 27] sts)

ALL SIZES

Rnd 3 [3, 3, 4, 4, 4, 4]: Ch 1, sc in same st, sk next sc, sc in each sc around, join in first sc. (18 [18, 20, 22, 22, 24, 26] sts)

Rnd 4 [4, 4, 5, 5, 5, 5]: Ch 1, sc in same st, ch 2 (counts as dc), dc in each st around, join in top of beg ch-2.

Rnd 5 [5, 5, 6, 6, 6, 6]: Fpsc (see Stitch Guide) around same st as join, ch 2 (counts as fpdc), fpdc (see Stitch Guide) around next st, join in top of beg ch-2.

Rnd 6 [6, 6, 7, 7, 7, 7]: Rep rnd 5 [5, 5, 6, 6, 6, 6].

CHILD SMALL, MEDIUM & LARGE SIZES ONLY

Fasten off.

ADULT SMALL, MEDIUM, LARGE & X-LARGE SIZES ONLY

Rnd [8, 8, 8, 8]: Rep rnd [6, 6, 6, 6]. Fasten off.

ALL SIZES

Rnd 8 [8, 8, 9, 9, 9, 9]: With A, join with fpsc around first fpdc of last rnd, ch 2, fpdc around, join in top of beg ch-2.

Rnd 9 [9, 9, 10, 10, 10, 10]: With C, rep rnd 8 [9], letting yarn A rem unused on WS.

Rnd 10 [10, 10, 11, 11, 11, 11]: With A, rep rnd 8 [9], letting yarn C rem unused on WS. Fasten off A.

Rnd 11 [11, 11, 12, 12, 12, 12]: Rep rnd 10 [11]. Fasten off.

HEEL TAB
CHILD SMALL, MEDIUM & LARGE SIZES ONLY

With 1 strand A, working in rem lps of rnd 4 of Sole in center back 5 sts at heel, join in first of 5 sts, sc in next st, 3 hdc in next st, sc in next st, join in next st. Fasten off.

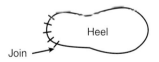

Track Shoes
Heel Tab Joining Diagram

ADULT SMALL, MEDIUM, LARGE & X-LARGE SIZES ONLY

With 1 strand A, working in rem lps of rnd 4 of Sole in center back 5 sts at heel, join in first of 5 sts, sc in next st, [2 hdc, dc, 2 hdc] in next st, sc in next, sl st in next st. Fasten off.

STRIPES ON SIDES
MAKE 8.

With single strand of A, ch 6 [6, 6, 8, 8, 8, 8], sc in 2nd st from hook and in each rem ch. Fasten off. Tack 2 Stripes to each side of each Shoe as shown in diagram.

Track Shoes
Stripes on Sides Placement Diagram

TOP PIECE OF SHOE

Row 1: Now working in rows, with B, ch 18 [18, 18, 20, 20, 22, 24], dc in 4th ch from hook, dc in each of next 3 [3, 3, 4, 4, 5, 6] sts, hdc in each of next 2 sts, 2 sc in each of next 3 sts, hdc in each of next 2 sts, dc in each of next 3 [3, 3, 4, 4, 5, 6] sts, **2-dc cl** (*see Special Stitch*) in last st, turn.

Row 2: Ch 2, sk cl st, dc in each of next 5 [5, 5, 6, 6, 7, 8] sts, 2 dc in each of next 2 sts, dc in each of next 2 sts, 2 dc in each of next 2 sts, dc in each of next 5 [5, 5, 6, 6, 7, 8] sts, ch 2, sl st in last st. Fasten off. Tack to top of Shoe at Instep.

TIES
MAKE 2.

With single strand of A, ch 70 [70, 75, 80, 80, 85, 90]. Lace ties through top piece (*see Lacing Diagram*).

FINISHING

Weave in all ends and remove stitch markers. ∎

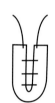

Track Shoes
Lacing Diagram

Ski Boots

SKILL LEVEL

INTERMEDIATE

FINISHED SIZES
Instructions given fit child's shoe size small (7–10); changes for child's medium (11–13) and large (1–3) and adult's small (women's 5–6), medium (women's 7–8), large (women's 9–10/men's 7–9) and X-large (men's 10–13) are in [ ].

FINISHED MEASUREMENTS
Sole: 6¾ [7½, 8½, 9, 9¾, 10½, 11¾] inches

MATERIALS
- Medium (worsted) weight yarn:
  5⅛ oz/260 yds/147g light blue (*A*)
  1½ oz/75 yds/43g bright pink (*B*)
  1⅜ oz/70 yds/40g yellow (*C*)
  1 oz/50 yds/28g white (*D*)
  ⅝ oz/35 yds20g green (*E*)

- Sizes H/8/5mm, I/9/5.5mm and J/10/6mm crochet hooks or size needed to obtain gauge
- Stitch marker
- Tapestry needle

GAUGE
Size H hook: 5 sc = 1¾ inches; 6 sc rows = 1¾ inches
Size I hook: 6 sc = 2 inches; 6 sc rows = 2 inches
Size J hook: 8 sc and 8 rows = 3 inches
Take time to check gauge.

PATTERN NOTES
Some sizes are achieved by changing the hook size, but the stitch count is the same as other sizes.

Boots are worked with 2 strands yarn held together throughout unless otherwise stated.

Divide each skein into two evenly sized hand-wound balls.

It will always look as if you are skipping a stitch or two at the end of each round. They are the joining slip stitch and chain-1. Do not work in these.

The stitch counts in [ ] may not always be in numerical sequence. These numbers are correct.

Join with slip stitch as indicated unless otherwise stated.

SPECIAL STITCHES
Spike stitch (spike st): Insert hook in base of indicated st 2 rows below, draw up lp of yarn to height of current row, yo, draw through 2 lps on hook.

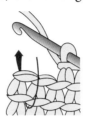

Spike Stitch

3-double crochet cluster (3-dc cl): Holding back on hook last lp of each st, 3 dc in indicated st or sp, yo, draw through all lps on hook.

SKI BOOT
MAKE 2.
SOLE
Rnd 1: With H [J, J, I, J, J, J] hook and with A, ch 13 [13, 15, 18, 18, 21, 24], 2 sc in 2nd ch from hook, sc in each of next 6 [6, 7, 9, 9, 11, 13] chs, dc in each of next 3 [3, 4, 5, 5, 6, 7] chs, 2 dc in next ch, 5 dc in end ch, mark center dc for toe, working in rem lps across opposite side of starting ch, 2 dc in next st, dc in each of next 3 [3, 4, 5, 5, 6, 7] sts, sc in each of next 7 [7, 8, 10, 10, 12, 14] sts, **join** (*see Pattern Notes*) in first sc. (*15 [15, 16, 21, 21, 25, 29] sc, 15 [15, 17, 19, 19, 21, 23] dc*)

CHILD SMALL, MEDIUM & LARGE AND ADULT SMALL & MEDIUM SIZES ONLY
Rnd 2 [2, 2, 2, 2]: Ch 1, sc in same st, 2 sc in next st, sc in each of next 12 [12, 14, 17, 17] sts, 2 sc in next st, 3 sc in next st, 2 sc in next st, sc in each of next 12 [12, 14, 17, 17] sts, 2 sc in next st, join in first sc. (*36 [36, 40, 46, 46] sc*)

ADULT LARGE & X-LARGE SIZES ONLY
Rnd [2, 2]: Ch 1, sc in same st, 2 sc in next st, sc in each of next [8, 9] sts, hdc in each of next [6, 7] sts, dc in each of next [6, 7] sts, 2 dc in next st, 3 dc in next st, 2 dc in next st, dc in each of next [6, 7] sts, hdc in each of next [6, 7] sts, sc in each of next [8, 9] sts, 2 sc in next st, join in first sc. (*[21, 23] sc, [12, 14] hdc, [19, 21] dc*)

ALL SIZES

Rnd 3 [3, 3, 3, 3, 3, 3]: Ch 1, sc in same st, 2 sc in next st, sc in each of next 12 [12, 14, 17, 17, 20, 23] sts, [2 sc in next st, sc in each of next 3 sts] twice, 2 sc in next st, sc in each of next 12 [12, 14, 17, 17, 20, 23] sts, 2 sc in next st, join in first sc. *(41 [41, 45, 51, 51, 57, 63] sts)*

BOOT
COLOR A BAND

Rnd 1: Continuing with A and working into **back lps** *(see Stitch Guide)* only for this rnd, ch 1, sc in same st, sc in each st around, join in first sc.

Rnd 2: Ch 1, sc in same st, sc in each of next 11 [11, 13, 16, 16, 16, 19] sts, sk next st, hdc in next st, dc in next st, [**dc dec** *(see Stitch Guide)* in next 2 sts, dc in next st] 2 [2, 2, 2, 2, 3, 3] times, [dc in next st, dc dec in next 2 sts] 2 [2, 2, 2, 2, 3, 3] times, dc in next st, hdc in next st, sk next st, sc in each of next 11 [11, 13, 16, 16, 16, 19] sts, join in first sc. *(35 [35, 39, 45, 45, 49, 55] sts)*

COLOR B BAND

Rnd 1: With B, ch 1, sc in same st, sc in each of next 11 [11, 13, 16, 16, 15, 18] sts, [dc dec in next 2 sts, dc in next st] 2 [2, 2, 2, 2, 3, 3] times, [dc in next st, dc dec in next 2 sts] 2 [2, 2, 2, 2, 3, 3] times, sc in each of next 11 [11, 13, 16, 16, 15, 18] sts, join in first sc. *(31 [31, 35, 41, 41, 43, 49] sts)*

Rnd 2: Ch 1, sc in same st, sc in each of next 9 [9, 11, 14, 14, 15, 18] sts, [dc dec in next 2 sts, dc in next st] twice, [dc in next st, dc dec in next 2 sts] twice, sc in each of next 9 [9, 11, 14, 14, 15, 18] sts, join in first sc. *(27 [27, 31, 37, 37, 39, 45] sts)*

CHILD SMALL, MEDIUM & LARGE SIZES ONLY
Fasten off.

ADULT SMALL, MEDIUM, LARGE & X-LARGE SIZES ONLY

Rnd [3, 3, 3, 3]: Ch 1, sc in same st, sc in each of next [12, 12, 13, 16] sts, [**sc dec** *(see Stitch Guide)* in next 2 sts, sc in next st] twice, [sc in next st, sc dec in next 2 sts] twice, sc in each of next [12, 12, 13, 16] sts, join in first sc. Fasten off. *([33, 35, 35, 41] sts)*

TRIM
With 2 strands D held tog and tapestry needle, overcast each rem lp of rnd 2 of Color A Band.

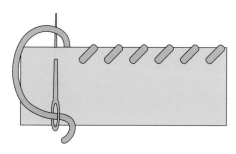

Overcast Stitch

COLOR C BAND

Rnd 1: With C, join with sc in fastened off st, sc in each of next 7 [7, 9, 10, 10, 11, 14] sts, [dc dec in next 2 sts, dc in next st] twice, [dc in next st, dc dec in next 2 sts] twice, sc in each of next 7 [7, 9, 10, 10, 11, 14] sts, join in first sc. *(23 [23, 27, 29, 29, 31, 37] sts)*

Rnd 2: Ch 1, sc in same st, sc in each of next 5 [5, 7, 8, 8, 9, 12] sts, [sc dec in next 2 sts, sc in next st] twice, [sc in next st, sc dec in next 2 sts] twice, sc in each of next 5 [5, 7, 8, 8, 9, 12] sts, join in first sc. Fasten off. *(19 [19, 23, 25, 25, 27, 33] sts)*

COLOR A BAND

Rnd 1: With A, join with sc in fastened off st, sk next st, **spike st** *(see Special Stitches)*, [sc in next st, spike st] around, join in first sc.

CHILD SMALL, MEDIUM & LARGE SIZES ONLY
Fasten off.

ADULT SMALL, MEDIUM, LARGE & X-LARGE SIZES ONLY

Rnd [2, 2, 2, 2]: Ch 1, sc in same st, sc in each st around, join in first sc. Fasten off.

COLOR D BAND
CHILD SMALL & MEDIUM SIZES ONLY

Rnd 1 [1]: With D, join with sc in fastened off st, sc in each st around, join in first sc.

Rnds 2 & 3 [2 & 3]: Ch 1, sc in same st, sc in each st around, join in first sc. Fasten off.

CHILD LARGE & ADULT SMALL, MEDIUM, LARGE & X-LARGE SIZES ONLY

Rnd [1, 1, 1, 1, 1]: With D, join with sc in fastened off st, sc in each of next [7, 8, 8, 9, 12] sts, sc dec in next 2 sts, sc in each of next 2 sts, sc dec in next 2 sts, sc in each of next [8, 9, 9, 10, 13] sts, join in first sc.

Rnds [2 & 3, 2 & 3, 2 & 3, 2 & 3, 2 & 3]: Ch 1, sc in same st, sc in each st around, join in first sc. At end of last row, fasten off Child Large.

ADULT X-LARGE SIZE ONLY

Rnd [2]: Ch 1, sc in same st, sc in each of next 12 sts, sc dec in next 2 sts, sc in each of next 2 sts, sc dec in next 2 sts, sc in each of next 12 sts, join in first sc. *([29] sts)*

Rnd [3]: Ch 1, sc in same st, sc in each of next 11 sts, sc dec in next 2 sts, sc in each of next 2 sts, sc dec in next 2 sts, sc in each of next 11 sts, join in first sc. *([27] sts)*

ADULT SMALL, MEDIUM, LARGE & X-LARGE SIZES ONLY

Rnd [4, 4, 4, 4]: Ch 1, sc in same st, sc in each sc around, join in first sc. Fasten off.

TRIM

With 2 strands C held tog, using **straight stitch** *(see illustration)*, embroider X's on middle rows of Color D Band.

Straight Stitch

COLOR E BAND

Rnd 1: With E, join with sc in fastened off st, **3-dc cl** *(see Special Stitches)* in next st, [sc in next st, 3-dc cl in next st] around, join in first sc. Fasten off.

COLOR A BAND 2

Rnd 1: With A, join with sc and sc in each st around, join in first sc.

Rnds 2 & 3 [2 & 3, 2 & 3, 2-4, 2-4, 2-4, 2-4]: Ch 1, sc in same st, sc in each sc around, join in first sc. At end of last row, fasten off.

TRIM

With double strand of B, embroider **French knots** *(see illustration)* on middle rows of Color D Band 2.

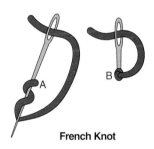

French Knot

COLOR C BAND 2

Rnd 1: With C, join with sc in fastened off st, 3-dc cl in next st, [sc in next st, 3-dc cl in next st] around, join with join in first sc. Fasten off.

COLOR A BAND 2

Rnd 1: With A, join with sc in fastened off st, sc in each st around, join in first sc. Fasten off.

TRIM ROUND

With one strand each A and D held together, join in fastened off st, **reverse sc** *(see Stitch Guide)* in same st, reverse sc in each st around, join in first sc. Fasten off. ∎

House Slippers

SKILL LEVEL

INTERMEDIATE

FINISHED SIZES

Instructions given fit child's shoe size small
(7–10); changes for child's medium (11–13),
large (1–3), and adult's small (women's 5–6),
medium (women's 7–8) and large (women's
9–10) are in [ ].

FINISHED MEASUREMENTS

Sole: 6¾ [7½, 8½, 9, 9¾, 10½] inches

MATERIALS

- Medium (worsted) weight yarn:
  5 oz/250 yds/142g light green
- Sizes H/8/5mm and J/10/6mm
  crochet hooks or size needed
  to obtain gauge
- Tapestry needle

4
MEDIUM

GAUGE

Size H hook: 5 sc = 1¾ inches; 6 sc rows = 1¾ inches
Size I hook: 6 sc = 2 inches; 6 sc rows = 2 inches
Size J hook: 8 sc and 8 rows = 3 inches
Take time to check gauge.

PATTERN NOTES

Some sizes are achieved by changing the hook
size, but the stitch count is the same as
other sizes.

Slippers are worked with 2 strands of yarn held
together throughout unless otherwise stated.

Chain-4 loops at the end of ruler rows form the
casing for the tie.

SPECIAL STITCH

Extended Chain (ext-ch): At beg of row, extend the
existing lp to the height of the following st.

SLIPPER

MAKE 2.

BODY

Row 1: With H [J, J, I, J, J] hook, ch 19 [19, 19,
21, 21, 22], sc in 5th ch from hook, sc in each
rem ch, turn. *(15 [15, 15, 17, 17, 18] sts)*

Row 2: Ch 4, working in **back lps** *(see Stitch
Guide)*, sc in each sc across, turn.

Rows 3–11 [3–11, 3–13, 3–13, 3–13, 3–15]: Rep row 2.

Row 12 [12, 14, 14, 14, 16]: Working in back lps, dc in each sc across, turn.

Row 13 [13, 15, 15, 15, 17]: Ext-ch (*see Special Stitch*), **bpdc** (*see Stitch Guide*) around next st across, turn.

Row 14 [14, 16, 16, 16, 18]: Ext-ch, **fpdc** (*see Stitch Guide*), across, turn.

Row 15 [15, 17, 17, 17, 19]: Ext-ch, bpdc around next st across, turn.

ADULT SMALL, MEDIUM & LARGE SIZES ONLY

Row [18, 18, 20]: Ext-ch, fpdc across, turn.

Row [19, 19, 21]: Ext-ch, bpdc across, turn.

ALL SIZES

Last row: Sk first dc, pull up lp in next st, [sk next st, pull up lp in next st] across, yo and pull through all lps on hook. Pull tight, ch 1 and fasten off.

Sew ends of dc rows together (*see Top Sewing Diagram*). Sew heel edge together (*see Heel Sewing Diagram*). Turn right side out.

House Slippers
Top Sewing Diagram

House Slippers
Heel Sewing Diagram

TIE

Ch 75, fasten off. Leaving long tail, thread through casing formed by ch-4 lps.

POMPOM
MAKE 4.

Cut two cardboard circles from pattern below. Cut 4 strands of yarn 30 inches long, thread 2 ends at a time in a tapestry needle. Holding the two cardboard circles together, wrap the cardboard with the yarn evenly around the circle as many times as possible. Thread the other 2 ends of the yarn in the tapestry needle and continue to wrap around. Insert the bottom tip of a pair of scissors between the two cardboard circles and carefully snip the yarn strands that are wrapping the cardboard. With a 10-inch strand of yarn, tie tightly between the circles. Wrap the core once more with the yarn for tie and tie firmly again. Remove cardboard circles and with longer tails of yarn, attach 1 Pompom to end of each Tie. Trim to desired length.

FINISHING

Weave in all ends. ■

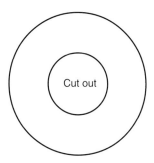

Cut out

Pompom Cardboard Circle

Tennis Socks

SKILL LEVEL

INTERMEDIATE

FINISHED SIZES

Instructions given fit child's shoe size small (7–10); changes for child's medium (11–13) and large (1–3) and adult's small (women's 5–6), medium (women's 7–8), large (women's 9–10/ men's 7–9) and X-large (men's 10–13) are in [ ].

FINISHED MEASUREMENTS

Sole: 6¾ [7½, 8½, 9, 9¾, 10½, 11¾] inches

MATERIALS

- Medium (worsted) weight yarn:
  3 oz/150 yds/85g white (B)
  2¼ oz/113 yds/64g lavender (A)
- Sizes H/8/5mm, I/9/5.5mm and J/10/6mm crochet hooks or size needed to obtain gauge
- Stitch marker
- Tapestry needle

GAUGE

Size H hook: 5 sc = 1¾ inches; 6 sc rows = 1¾ inches
Size I hook: 6 sc = 2 inches; 6 sc rows = 2 inches
Size J hook: 8 sc and 8 rows = 3 inches
Take time to check gauge.

PATTERN NOTES

Some sizes are achieved by changing the hook size, but the stitch count is the same as other sizes.

Socks are worked with 2 strands held together throughout unless otherwise stated.

Divide each skein into two evenly sized hand-wound balls.

It will always look as if you are skipping a stitch or two at the end of each round. They are the joining slip stitch and chain-1. Do not work in these.

The stitch counts in [ ] may not always be in numerical sequence. These numbers are correct.

Join with slip stitch as indicated unless otherwise stated.

SPECIAL STITCH

Spike stitch (spike st): Insert hook in base of indicated st 2 rows below, draw up lp of yarn to height of current row, yo, draw through 2 lps on hook.

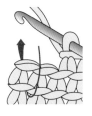

Spike Stitch

TENNIS SOCK
MAKE 2.
SOLE
Rnd 1: With H [J, J, I, J, J, J] hook and with A, ch 13 [13, 15, 18, 18, 21, 24], 2 sc in 2nd ch from hook, sc in each of next 6 [6, 7, 9, 9, 11, 13] chs, dc in each of next 3 [3, 4, 5, 5, 6, 7] chs, 2 dc in next ch, 5 dc in end ch, mark center dc for toe, working in rem lps across opposite side of starting ch, 2 dc in next st, dc in each of next 3 [3, 4, 5, 5, 6, 7] sts, sc in each of next 7 [7, 8, 10, 10, 12, 14] sts, **join** (*see Pattern Notes*) in first sc. (*15 [15, 16, 21, 21, 25, 29] sc, 15 [15, 17, 19, 19, 21, 23] dc*)

CHILD SMALL, MEDIUM, LARGE SIZES & ADULT SMALL & MEDIUM SIZES ONLY
Rnd 2 [2, 2, 2, 2]: Ch 1, sc in same st, 2 sc in next st, sc in each of next 12 [12, 14, 17, 17] sts, 2 sc in next st, 3 sc in next st, 2 sc in next st, sc in each of next 12 [12, 14, 17, 17] sts, 2 sc in next st, join in first sc. (*36 [36, 40, 46, 46] sc*)

ADULT LARGE & X-LARGE SIZES ONLY
Rnd [2, 2]: Ch 1, sc in same st as beg ch-1, 2 sc in next st, sc in each of next [8, 9] sts, hdc in each of next [6, 7] sts, dc in each of next [6, 7] sts, 2 dc in next st, 3 dc in next st, 2 dc in next st, dc in each of next [6, 7] sts, hdc in each of next [6, 7] sts, sc in each of next [8, 9] sts, 2 sc in next st, join in first sc. (*[21, 23] sc, [12, 14] hdc, [19, 21] dc*)

ALL SIZES
Rnd 3 [3, 3, 3, 3, 3, 3]: Ch 1, sc in same st, 2 sc in next st, sc in each of next 12 [12, 14, 17, 17, 20, 23] sts, [2 sc in next st, sc in each of next 3 sts] twice, 2 sc in next st, sc in each of next 12 [12, 14, 17, 17, 20, 23] sts, 2 sc in next st, join in first sc. Fasten off. (*41 [41, 45, 51, 51, 57, 63] sts*)

TOP
Rnd 1: With B, join with sc in **back lp** (*see Stitch Guide*) of fastened off st from previous rnd, continue working in back lps only, sc in each of next 17 [17, 18, 20, 20, 22, 24] sts, hdc in each of next 6 [6, 8, 10, 10, 12, 14] sts, dc in each of next 17 [17, 18, 20, 20, 22, 24] sts, join in first sc.

Rnd 2: Ch 1, sc in same st, sc in each of next 11 [11, 13, 16, 16, 16, 19] sts, sk next st, hdc in next st, dc in next st, [**dc dec** (*see Stitch Guide*) in next 2 sts, dc in next st] 2 [2, 2, 2, 2, 3, 3] times, [dc in next st, dc dec in next 2 sts] 2 [2, 2, 2, 2, 3, 3] times, dc in next st, hdc in next st, sk next st, sc in each of next 11 [11, 13, 16, 16, 16, 19] sts, join in first sc. (*35 [35, 39, 45, 45, 49, 55] sts*)

Rnd 3: Ch 1, sc in same st, sc in each of next 11 [11, 13, 16, 16, 15, 18] sts, [dc dec in next 2 sts, dc in next st] 2 [2, 2, 2, 2, 3, 3] times, [dc in next st, dc dec in next 2 sts] 2 [2, 2, 2, 2, 3, 3] times, sc in each of next 11 [11, 13, 16, 16, 15, 18] sts, join in first sc. (*31 [31, 35, 41, 41, 43, 49] sts*)

Rnd 4: Ch 1, sc in same st, sc in each of next 9 [9, 11, 14, 14, 15, 18] sts, [dc dec in next 2 sts, dc in next st] twice, [dc in next st, dc dec in next 2 sts] twice, sc in each of next 9 [9, 11, 14, 14, 15, 18] sts, join in first sc. (*27 [27, 31, 37, 37, 39, 45] sts*)

Rnd 5: Ch 1, sc in same st, sc in each of next 7 [7, 9, 12, 12, 13, 16] sts, [dc dec in next 2 sts, dc in next st] twice, [dc in next st, dc dec in next 2 sts] twice, sc in each of next 7 [7, 9, 12, 12, 13, 16] sts, join in first sc. (*23 [23, 27, 33, 33, 35, 41] sts*)

CHILD SMALL, MEDIUM & LARGE SIZES ONLY
Rnd 6 [6, 6]: Ch 1, sc in same st, sc in each of next 5 [5, 7] sts, [**sc dec** (*see Stitch Guide*) in next 2 sts, sc in next st] twice, [sc in next st, sc dec in next 2 sts] twice, sc in each of next 5 [5, 7] sts, join in first sc. Fasten off. (*19 [19, 23] sts*)

ADULT SMALL, MEDIUM, LARGE & X-LARGE SIZES ONLY
Rnd [6, 6, 6, 6]: Ch 1, sc in same st, sc in each of next [10, 10, 11, 14] sts, sc dec in next 2 sts, dc in next st, dc dec in next 2 sts, dc in each of next 2 sts, dc dec in next 2 sts, dc in next st, sc dec in next 2 sts, sc in each of next [10, 10, 11, 14] sts, join in first sc. (*[29, 29, 31, 37] sts*)

Rnd [7, 7, 7, 7]: Ch 1, sc in same st, sc in each of next [8, 8, 9, 12] sts, [sc dec in next 2 sts, sc in next st] twice, [sc in next st, sc dec in next 2 sts] twice, sc in each of next [8, 8, 9, 12] sts, join in first sc. Fasten off. (*[25, 25, 27, 33] sts*)

TRIM

With A, join with sc in fastened off st from previous row, [**spike st** *(see Special Stitch)*, sc] around, join with sl st to first sc. Fasten off.

POMPOM
MAKE 2.

Cut two cardboard circles from pattern below. Cut 4 strands of B 30 inches long, thread 2 ends at a time in a tapestry needle. Holding the two cardboard circles together, wrap the cardboard with the yarn evenly around the circle as many times as possible. Thread the other 2 ends of the yarn in the tapestry needle and continue to wrap around. Insert the bottom tip of a pair of scissors between the two cardboard circles and carefully snip the yarn strands that are wrapping the cardboard. With a 10-inch strand of yarn, tie tightly between the circles. Wrap the core once more with the yarn for tie and

tie firmly again. Remove cardboard circles and with longer tails of yarn, tack 1 Pompom to back of each Sock.

Trim to taste.

FINISHING

Weave in all ends and remove stitch marker. ∎

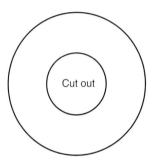

Pompom Cardboard Circle

Work Boots

SKILL LEVEL

INTERMEDIATE

FINISHED SIZES

Instructions given fit child's shoe size small
(7–10); changes for child's medium (11–13),
large (1–3), and adult's small (women's 5–6),
medium (women's 7–8), large (women's 9–10/
men's 7–9) and X-large (men's 10–13) are in [ ].

FINISHED MEASUREMENTS

Sole: 6¾ [7½, 8½, 9, 9¾, 10½, 11¾] inches

MATERIALS

- Medium (worsted) weight yarn:
  5 oz/250 yds/142g medium
  brown (A)
  2½ oz/130 yds/74g tan (B)
  ⅛ oz/6 yds/4g dark brown (C)
- Sizes H/8/5mm, I/9/5.5mm and J/10/6mm
  crochet hooks or size needed to obtain gauge
- Stitch marker
- Tapestry needle

GAUGE

Size H hook: 5 sc = 1¾ inches; 6 sc rows =
1¾ inches
Size I hook: 6 sc = 2 inches; 6 sc rows = 2 inches
Size J hook: 8 sc and 8 rows = 3 inches
Take time to check gauge.

PATTERN NOTES

Some sizes are achieved by changing the hook size,
but the stitch count is the same as other sizes.

Boots are worked with 2 strands held together
throughout unless otherwise stated.

Divide each skein into two evenly sized hand-
wound balls.

It will always look as if you are skipping a stitch
or two at the end of each round. They are the
joining slip stitch and chain-1. Do not work
in these.

The stitch counts in [ ] may not always be in
numerical sequence. These numbers are correct.

Join with slip stitch as indicated unless
otherwise stated.

WORK BOOT
MAKE 2.
SOLE

Rnd 1: With H [J, J, I, J, J, J] hook and with A, ch
13 [13, 15, 18, 18, 21, 24], 2 sc in 2nd ch from
hook, sc in each of next 6 [6, 7, 9, 9, 11, 13] chs,
dc in each of next 3 [3, 4, 5, 5, 6, 7] chs, 2 dc
in next ch, 5 dc in end ch, mark center dc for
toe, working in rem lps across opposite side of
starting ch, 2 dc in next st, dc in each of next 3
[3, 4, 5, 5, 6, 7] sts, sc in each of next 7 [7, 8, 10,
10, 12, 14] sts, **join** (see Pattern Notes) in first
sc. (15 [15, 16, 21, 21, 25, 29] sc, 15 [15, 17, 19,
19, 21, 23] dc)

CHILD SMALL, MEDIUM & LARGE AND ADULT SMALL & MEDIUM SIZES ONLY

Rnd 2 [2, 2, 2, 2]: Ch 1, sc in same st, 2 sc in
next st, sc in each of next 12 [12, 14, 17, 17] sts,
2 sc in next st, 3 sc in next st, 2 sc in next st,
sc in each of next 12 [12, 14, 17, 17] sts, 2 sc in
next st, join in first sc. (36 [36, 40, 46, 46] sc)

ADULT LARGE & X-LARGE SIZES ONLY

Rnd [2, 2]: Ch 1, sc in same st, 2 sc in next st, sc
in each of next [8, 9] sts, hdc in each of next [6,
7] sts, dc in each of next [6, 7] sts, 2 dc in next
st, 3 dc in next st, 2 dc in next st, dc in each of
next [6, 7] sts, hdc in next [6, 7] sts, sc in each
of next [8, 9] sts, 2 sc in next st, join in first sc.
([21, 23] sc, [12, 14] hdc, [19, 21] dc)

ALL SIZES

Rnd 3 [3, 3, 3, 3, 3]: Ch 1, sc in same st, 2 sc
in next st, sc in each of next 12 [12, 14, 17, 17,
20, 23] sts, [2 sc in next st, sc in each of next 3
sts] twice, 2 sc in next st, sc in each of next 12
[12, 14, 17, 17, 20, 23] sts, 2 sc in next st, join in
first sc. (41 [41, 45, 51, 51, 57, 63] sts)

BOOT

Rnd 1: Working in **back lps** (see Stitch Guide) or this
rnd, and with A, join at fasten off from previous
rnd, ch 1, sc in each sc around, join in first sc.

Rnd 2 [2, 2, 2-3, 2-3, 2-3, 2-3]: Ch 1, sc in
same st, sc in each sc around, join in first sc.

Rnd 3 [3, 3, 4, 4, 4, 4]: Ch 1, sc in same st,
sc in each of next 14 [14, 16, 19, 19, 19, 22] sc,
[**sc dec** (see Stitch Guide) in next 2 sts, sc in
next sc] 2 [2, 2, 2, 2, 3, 3] times, [sc in next sc,

sc dec in next 2 sts] 2 [2, 2, 2, 2, 3, 3] times, sc in each of next 14 [14, 16, 19, 19, 19, 22] sc, join in first sc. Fasten off. *(37 [37, 41, 47, 47, 51, 57] sts)*

INSTEP
Row 1: Now working in rows, with A, working in back lps only, sk next 12 [12, 14, 17, 17, 18, 20] sts after where you just fastened off, join in next st, [sc dec in next 2 sts] 5 [5, 5, 5, 5, 6, 6] times, sl st in next st, turn. *(5 [5, 5, 5, 5, 6, 6] sts)*

CHILD SMALL, MEDIUM & LARGE SIZES ONLY
Row 2 [2, 2]: Sk sl st, sc in next st, [sk next sc, sc in next sc] twice, sl st in inside lp of next st on Boot, turn. *(3 [3, 3] sc)*

ADULT SMALL & MEDIUM SIZES ONLY
Row [2, 2]: Sk sl st, sc in each of next 5 sc, sl st in inside lp of next st on Boot, turn. *([5, 5] sc)*

ADULT LARGE & X-LARGE ADULT SIZES ONLY
Row [2, 2]: Sk sl st, sc in each of next 2 sc, sk next st, sc in each of next 3 sc, sl st in inside lp of next st on Boot, turn. *([5, 5] sc)*

ALL SIZES
Rows 3–5 [3–5, 3–5, 3–10, 3–10, 3–10, 3–12]: Sk sl st, sc in each of next 3 [3, 3, 5, 5, 5, 5] sc, sl st in inside lp of next st on Boot, turn. **Do not fasten off.**

TONGUE
Row 1: Ch 1, sc in first sc, 2 sc in next sc, sc in each of next 1 [1, 1, 3, 3, 3, 3] st(s), turn.

Rows 2–8 [2–8, 2–8, 2–11, 2–11, 2–11, 2–11]: Ch 1, sc in each of next 4 [4, 4, 6, 6, 6, 6] sts, turn. Fasten off.

BOOT SIDES
Row 1: With toe of Boot toward you, and working with A, sc to join in rem lp of st on left side where last row of Instep joined to Boot side, sc in both lps of each of next 21 [21, 26, 27, 27, 30, 32] sts, sc in remaining lp of next st, turn. *(23 [23, 28, 29, 29, 32, 34] sts)*

Rows 2–4: Ch 1, sk first sc, sc in each st across to last 2 sts, sk next st, sc in last, turn. *(17 [17, 22, 23, 23, 26, 28] sts at end of last row)*

Rows 5–7: Ch 1, sc in each sc, turn. Fasten off.

Row 8: With B, join with sc at heel and sc in each sc of last row. Fasten off.

RIDGE AROUND SOLE
With B and working in rem lps of last rnd of Sole and with Sole facing away, join with sl st at center back of heel, sl st loosely in each st around, join in first sl st. Fasten off.

TRIM
With single strand of B and tapestry needle, embroider stitching lines on sides *(see illustration)* and **overcast stitches** *(see illustration)* around Instep.

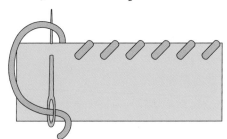

Overcast Stitch

Work Boots
Trim Diagram

SHOE STRINGS
MAKE 2.
With single strand of dark brown, ch 100 [100, 105, 110, 110, 115, 120]. Fasten off and tie. Lace into front edges.

FINISHING
Weave in all ends and remove stitch markers. ∎

Mary Janes

SKILL LEVEL

INTERMEDIATE

FINISHED SIZES

Instructions given fit child's shoe size small
(7–10); changes for child's medium (11–13),
large (1–3), and adult's small (women's 5–6),
medium (women's 7–8) and large (women's
9–10) are in [ ].

FINISHED MEASUREMENTS

Sole: 6¾ [7¼, 8½, 9, 9¾, 10½] inches

MATERIALS

- Medium (worsted) weight yarn:
  3⅝ oz/181 yds/103g white *(B)*
  3½ oz/175 yds/99g black *(A)*
- Sizes H/8/5mm, I/9/5.5mm and
  J/10/6mm crochet hooks or size
  needed to obtain gauge
- 3 stitch markers
- Tapestry needle

GAUGE

Size H hook: 5 sc = 1¾ inches; 6 sc rows =
  1¾ inches
Size I hook: 6 sc = 2 inches; 6 sc rows = 2 inches
Size J hook: 8 sc and 8 rows = 3 inches
Take time to check gauge.

PATTERN NOTES

Some sizes are achieved by changing the hook size,
  but the stitch count is the same as other sizes.

Slippers are worked with 2 strands held together
  throughout unless otherwise stated.

Divide each skein into two evenly sized hand-
  wound balls.

It will always look as if you are skipping a stitch or
  two at the end of each round. They are the joining slip stitch and chain-1. Do not work in these.

The stitch counts in [ ] may not always be in
  numerical sequence. These numbers are correct.

Join with slip stitch as indicated unless otherwise stated.

SPECIAL STITCH

3-dc cluster (3-dc cl): 3 dc in 1 st, do not work off last lp of each st, yo, and pull through all lps on hook.

MARY JANE
MAKE 2.
SOLE

Rnd 1: With H [J, J, I, J, J] hook and with A, ch 13 [13, 15, 18, 18, 21], 2 sc in 2nd ch from hook, sc in each of next 6 [6, 7, 9, 9, 11] chs, dc in each of next 3 [3, 4, 5, 5, 6] chs, 2 dc in next ch, 5 dc in end ch, mark center dc for toe, working in rem lps across opposite side of starting ch, 2 dc in next st, dc in each of next 3 [3, 4, 5, 5, 6] sts, sc in each of next 7 [7, 8, 10, 10, 12] sts, **join** (*see Pattern Notes*) in first sc. (*15 [15, 17, 21, 21, 25] sc, 15 [15, 17, 19, 19, 21] dc*)

CHILD SMALL, MEDIUM, LARGE AND ADULT SMALL & MEDIUM SIZES ONLY

Rnd 2 [2, 2, 2, 2]: Ch 1, sc in same st, 2 sc in next st, sc in each of next 12 [12, 14, 17, 17] sts, 2 sc in next st, 3 sc in next st, 2 sc in next st, sc in each of next 12 [12, 14, 17, 17] sts, 2 sc in next st, join in first sc. (*36 [36, 40, 46, 46] sc*)

ADULT LARGE SIZE ONLY

Rnd [2]: Ch 1, sc in same st, 2 sc in next st, sc in each of next 8 sts, hdc in each of next 6 sts, dc in each of next 6 sts, 2 dc in next st, 3 dc in next st, 2 dc in next st, dc in each of next 6 sts, hdc in each of next 6 sts, sc in each of next 8 sts, 2 sc in next st, join in first sc. (*[21] sc, [12] hdc, [19] dc*)

ALL SIZES

Rnd 3 [3, 3, 3, 3]: Ch 1, sc in same st, 2 sc in next st, sc in each of next 12 [12, 14, 17, 17, 20] sts, [2 sc in next st, sc in each of next 3 sts] twice, 2 sc in next st, sc in each of next 12 [12, 14, 17, 17, 20] sts, 2 sc in next st, join in first sc. (*41 [41, 45, 51, 51, 57] sts*)

SHOE

Rnds 4 & 5 [4 & 5, 4 & 5, 4 & 5, 4 & 5, 4 & 5]: Working in **back lps** (*see Stitch Guide*) for this rnd, ch 1, sc in same st, sc in each sc around, join in first sc.

CHILD SMALL, MEDIUM & LARGE SIZES ONLY

Rnd 6 [6, 6]: Ch 1, sc in same st, sc in each of next 14 [14, 13] sts, [**sc dec** (*see Stitch Guide*) in next 2 sts, sc in next st] 2 [2, 3] times, [sc in next st, sc dec in next 2 sts] 2 [2, 3] times, sc in each of next 14 [14, 13] sts, join in first sc. (*37 [37, 39] sts*)

Rnd 7 [7, 7]: Ch 1, sc in same st, sc in each of next 13 [13, 14] sts, [sc dec in next 2 sts] 5 [5, 5] times, sc in each of next 13 [13, 14] sts, join in first sc. Fasten off. (*32 [32, 34] sts*)

ADULT SMALL, MEDIUM & LARGE SIZES ONLY

Rnd [6, 6, 6]: Ch 1, sc in same st, sc in each of next [16, 16, 19] sts, **sc dec** (*see Stitch Guide*) in next 2 sts, dc in next st, [**dc dec** (*see Stitch Guide*) in next 2 sts, dc in next st] twice, [dc in next st, dc dec in next 2 sts] twice, dc in next st, sc dec in next 2 sts, sc in each of next [16, 16, 19] sts, join in first sc. (*[45, 45, 51] sts*)

Rnd [7, 7, 7]: Ch 1, sc in same st, sc in each of next [17, 17, 18] sts, [dc dec in next 2 sts] [5, 5, 7] times, sc in each of next [17, 17, 18] sts, join in first sc. Fasten off. (*[40, 40, 44] sts*)

STOCKING INSTEP
ALL SIZES

Row 1: Now working in rows, locate center 8 [8, 8, 9, 9, 9] sts of toe end of last rnd with toe facing you, with B, join in back lp of the first st, sk next st, sc in back lp of each of next 4 [4, 4, 5, 5, 5] sts, sk next st, join in back lp of next st, turn.

Rows 2–8 [2–8, 2–8, 2–9, 2–9, 2–11]: Sk sl st, sc in each of next 4 [4, 4, 5, 5, 5] sts, join in back lp of next st on side of Shoe, turn. Fasten off on last row.

STOCKING ANKLE

Rnd 1: Now working in rnds, with B, join with sc in back lp on last rnd of Shoe at heel, sc in back lp of each st on Shoe to Instep, place marker, sc in each of next 4 [4, 4, 5, 5, 5] sts across Instep, place marker, sc in back lp of each rem st on Shoe, join in first sc. (*21 [21, 23, 28, 28, 30] sts*)

Rnd 2: Ch 1, sc in same st, sc in each st around, working sc dec in marked st and next st on each side of Instep, sl st to first sc to join, move markers to top of respective sts. *(19 [19, 21, 26, 26, 28] sts)*

CHILD SMALL, MEDIUM & LARGE SIZES ONLY

Rnd 3 [3, 3]: Ch 1, sc in same st, sc in each st around, sl st to first sc.

ADULT SMALL, MEDIUM, LARGE & X-LARGE SIZES ONLY

Rnds [3 & 4, 3 & 4, 3 & 4, 3 & 4]: Rep rnd 2. *(22 [22, 24] sts)*

ALL SIZES

Rnd 5 [5, 5, 5, 5, 5]: Working in back lps only for this rnd, ch 1, sc in same st, ch 2, dc in each st around, join in top of ch-2. *(19 [19, 21, 22, 22, 24] sts)*

Rnd 6 [6, 6, 6, 6, 6]: Ch 2, **fpsc** *(see Stitch Guide)*, ch 2, **fpdc** *(see Stitch Guide)* around, join in top of beg ch-2.

Rnds 7 & 8 [7 & 8, 7 & 8, 7–10, 7–10, 7–10]: Rep rnd 6. Fasten off.

STOCKING TRIM

Working in rem lps of rnd 3 [3, 3, 4, 4, 4] of Stocking, with single strand of B, join with sc, ch 2, [sc in next st, ch 2] around, join in first st. Fasten off.

ANKLE STRAP

With single strand of A, join with sc to lp on top edge of inside of Shoe, ch 8 [8, 8, 10, 10, 10], sl st to lp on other side, ch 3, **3-dc cl** *(see Special Stitch)* in 3rd ch from hook, join in same ch, sc in each rem ch, join in first sc. Fasten off.

Rep on rem Shoe.

FINISHING

Weave in all ends and remove stitch markers. ∎

Big Foot Boutique is published by DRG, 306 East Parr Road, Berne, IN 46711. Printed in USA. Copyright © 2011 DRG. All rights reserved. This publication may not be reproduced in part or in whole without written permission from the publisher.

RETAIL STORES: If you would like to carry this pattern book or any other DRG publications, visit DRGwholesale.com.

Every effort has been made to ensure that the instructions in this publication are complete and accurate. We cannot, however, take responsibility for human error, typographical mistakes or variations in individual work. Please visit AnniesCustomerCare.com to check for pattern updates.

ISBN: 978-1-59635-399-2

3 4 5 6 7 8 9

STITCH GUIDE

STITCH ABBREVIATIONS

beg	begin/begins/beginning
bpdc	back post double crochet
bpsc	back post single crochet
bptr	back post treble crochet
CC	contrasting color
ch(s)	chain(s)
ch-	refers to chain or space previously made (i.e., ch-1 space)
ch sp(s)	chain space(s)
cl(s)	cluster(s)
cm	centimeter(s)
dc	double crochet (singular/plural)
dc dec	double crochet 2 or more stitches together, as indicated
dec	decrease/decreases/decreasing
dtr	double treble crochet
ext	extended
fpdc	front post double crochet
fpsc	front post single crochet
fptr	front post treble crochet
g	gram(s)
hdc	half double crochet
hdc dec	half double crochet 2 or more stitches together, as indicated
inc	increase/increases/increasing
lp(s)	loop(s)
MC	main color
mm	millimeter(s)
oz	ounce(s)
pc	popcorn(s)
rem	remain/remains/remaining
rep(s)	repeat(s)
rnd(s)	round(s)
RS	right side
sc	single crochet (singular/plural)
sc dec	single crochet 2 or more stitches together, as indicated
sk	skip/skipped/skipping
sl st(s)	slip stitch(es)
sp(s)	space(s)/spaced
st(s)	stitch(es)
tog	together
tr	treble crochet
trtr	triple treble
WS	wrong side
yd(s)	yard(s)
yo	yarn over

YARN CONVERSION

OUNCES TO GRAMS		GRAMS TO OUNCES	
1	28.4	25	⅞
2	56.7	40	1⅔
3	85.0	50	1¾
4	113.4	100	3½

UNITED STATES		UNITED KINGDOM
sl st (slip stitch)	=	sc (single crochet)
sc (single crochet)	=	dc (double crochet)
hdc (half double crochet)	=	htr (half treble crochet)
dc (double crochet)	=	tr (treble crochet)
tr (treble crochet)	=	dtr (double treble crochet)
dtr (double treble crochet)	=	ttr (triple treble crochet)
skip	=	miss

Reverse single crochet (reverse sc): Ch 1, sk first st, working from left to right, insert hook in next st from front to back, draw up lp on hook, yo, and draw through both lps on hook.

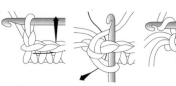

Chain (ch): Yo, pull through lp on hook.

Single crochet (sc): Insert hook in st, yo, pull through st, yo, pull through both lps on hook.

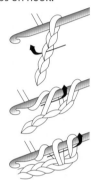

Double crochet (dc): Yo, insert hook in st, yo, pull through st, [yo, pull through 2 lps] twice.

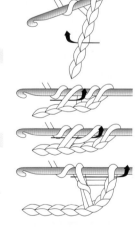

Front loop (front lp) Back loop (back lp)

Front Loop   Back Loop

Front post stitch (fp): Back post stitch (bp): When working post st, insert hook from right to left around post of st on previous row.

Back   Front

Post of Stitch

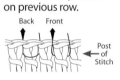

Half double crochet (hdc): Yo, insert hook in st, yo, pull through st, yo, pull through all 3 lps on hook.

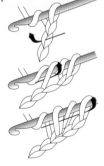

Double treble crochet (dtr): Yo 3 times, insert hook in st, yo, pull through st, [yo, pull through 2 lps] 4 times.

Slip stitch (sl st): Insert hook in st, pull through both lps on hook.

Chain color change (ch color change) Yo with new color, draw through last lp on hook.

Double crochet color change (dc color change) Drop first color, yo with new color, draw through last 2 lps of st.

Treble crochet (tr): Yo twice, insert hook in st, yo, pull through st, [yo, pull through 2 lps] 3 times.

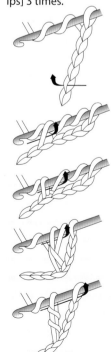

Single crochet decrease (sc dec): (Insert hook, yo, draw lp through) in each of the sts indicated, yo, draw through all lps on hook.

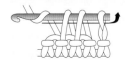

Example of 2-sc dec

Half double crochet decrease (hdc dec): (Yo, insert hook, yo, draw lp through) in each of the sts indicated, yo, draw through all lps on hook.

Example of 2-hdc dec

Double crochet decrease (dc dec): (Yo, insert hook, yo, draw lp through, yo, draw through 2 lps on hook) in each of the sts indicated, yo, draw through all lps on hook.

Example of 2-dc dec

Treble crochet decrease (tr dec): Holding back last lp of each st, tr in each of the sts indicated, yo, pull through all lps on hook.

Example of 2-tr dec